BLAZERS

TOP 10
UNEXPLAINED

Top 10

UNSOLVED
mysteries

by Kathryn Clay

Content Consultant:
Dr. Andrew Nichols
Director of the
American Institute of Parapsychology
Gainesville, Florida

Reading Consultant:
Barbara J. Fox
Reading Specialist
Professor Emeritus
North Carolina State University

CAPSTONE PRESS
a capstone imprint

Blazers is published by Capstone Press,
1710 Roe Crest Drive, North Mankato, Minnesota 56003.
www.capstonepub.com

Books published by Capstone Press are manufactured with paper
containing at least 10 percent post-consumer waste.

Library of Congress Cataloging-in-Publication Data
Clay, Kathryn.
    Top 10 unsolved mysteries / by Kathryn Clay.
    p. cm. — (Top 10 unexplained)
    Summary: "Describes various unsolved mysteries throughout history in a top-ten format"
—Provided by publisher.
    Includes bibliographical references and index.
    ISBN 978-1-4296-7637-3 (hardcover)
    1. Curiosities and wonders—Juvenile literature. I. Title. II. Title: Top ten unsolved mysteries.
AG243.C566 2012
001.94—dc23   2011034690

Editorial Credits
Mandy Robbins, editor; Veronica Correia, designer; Eric Gohl, media researcher;
    Laura Manthe, production specialist

Photo Credits
Alamy/Everett Collection Inc, 23 (front); North Wind Picture Archives, 27
Bridgeman Art Library/© Look and Learn/Private Collection, 9
Corbis/Bettmann, 23 (back)
Dreamstime/Yaroslava Polosina, 11
Granger Collection, NYC, 21, 25
iStockphoto/Andrew Rich, 7; Joze Pojbic, 15
Shutterstock/Carles Fortuny, 13; faberfoto, 17; Filip Fuxa, cover, 5;
IND. mangojuicy, 29
Wikipedia, 19

Printed in the United States of America in Stevens Point, Wisconsin.
102011   006404WZS12

TABLE OF CONTENTS

STUBBORN MYSTERIES

Science has solved many mysteries in modern times. But some stubborn mysteries remain. From strange creatures to sudden disappearances, check out today's top 10 mysteries.

BIGFOOT

For hundreds of years, American Indian **legends** told of giant, apelike creatures. People continue to report seeing these animals wandering the forests of North America. Do bigfoots really exist? Or are the reports just **hoaxes**?

legend–a story handed down from earlier times
hoax–a trick to make people believe something that is not true

People in Asia claim to have seen apelike creatures in the Himalayan Mountains. They call the beasts "yetis."

LOCH NESS MONSTER

Many witnesses have seen something poke out of **Loch** Ness in Scotland. People have reported a creature with a long neck and several humps gliding through the water. Is it the Loch Ness monster? So far scientists cannot prove the sea monster is real.

FACT According to legend, Saint Columba reported the first Loch Ness monster sighting in the year 565.

loch–the Scottish word for lake

8

STONEHENGE

Stonehenge is a circle of giant stones that stands in southwestern England. Some people believe Stonehenge is an ancient church, graveyard, or huge calendar. No one knows for sure.

FACT Researchers wonder how the heavy stones were moved. Some stones weigh more than 25 tons (23 metric tons).

MACHU PICCHU

Around 1450 the Incas built a secret city in the Andes Mountains of Peru. The secrect city is called Machu Picchu. Hiram Bingham found the **ruins** in 1911. But no one has ever figured out why the city was left empty.

10
9
8
7
6
5
4

ruins—the remains of something that has collapsed or been destroyed

CROP CIRCLES

All over the world, patterns appear in farmers' fields. In some cases, people admit to making them. But not all crop circles have been explained. Some people think aliens make the designs.

NAZCA LINES

Large pictures are carved into the Nazca Desert of Peru. These drawings can only be seen from the air. Are the Nazca lines more signs of aliens among us?

FACT Many scientists believe Nazca Indians made the lines more than 2,000 years ago.

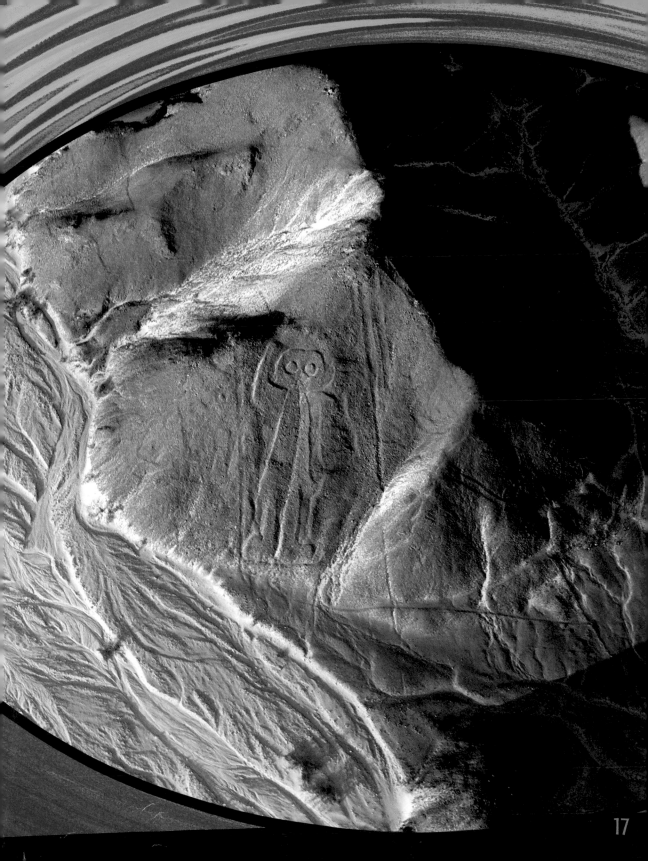

AMELIA EARHART

In 1937 Amelia Earhart tried to become the first woman to fly around the world. She almost made it, but her plane ran out of fuel. Earhart and her copilot, Fred Noonan, disappeared without a trace.

FACT Some researchers believe Earhart and Noonan crashed on a remote island in the Pacific Ocean.

BERMUDA TRIANGLE

More than 100 planes and ships have vanished in the **Bermuda Triangle**. Maybe storms or equipment failure caused them to go down. Or perhaps something more mysterious is to blame for the disappearances.

Bermuda Triangle–an area in the Atlantic Ocean bounded by Bermuda, Puerto Rico, and Florida where ships and airplanes have mysteriously disappeared

D.B. COOPER

10

9

8

7

6

5

4

D. B. Cooper **hijacked** a plane and demanded thousands of dollars. After he received the money, he jumped out of the moving plane. Some of the money was found. But Cooper was never seen again.

2

hijack—to take illegal control of a vehicle

An 8-year-old boy found $5,800 stolen by D. B. Cooper near a stream in Washington.

FBI SKETCH OF
D.B. COOPER

ROANOKE COLONY

Roanoke Island, Virginia, was the site of the first English **colony** in North America. Settlers built a village there in 1585. They survived by trading with the American Indians for food. But their friendship with the Indians didn't last.

colony—a large area that has been settled by people from another country

Perhaps the settlers starved to death. Or maybe the American Indians killed them. When rescuers from England arrived, the settlers were gone. All that was found was the word "CROATOAN" carved into a tree.

FACT Many people believe the colonists fled to Croatoan Island. But they were never found there either.

SEEKING ANSWERS

It's never too late to study unsolved mysteries. People continue to search for clues and look for answers. Perhaps one day some of these mysteries will be solved.

Glossary

alien (AY-lee-uhn)—a creature not from Earth

ancient (AYN-shunt)—belonging to a time long ago

Bermuda Triangle (bur-MYOO-duh TRY-ang-guhl)—an area in the Atlantic Ocean bounded by Bermuda, Puerto Rico, and Florida where ships and airplanes have disappeared

colony (KAH-luh-nee)—a large area that has been settled by people from another country

hijack (HYE-jak)—to take illegal control of a vehicle

hoax (HOHKS)—a trick to make people believe something that is not true

legend (LEJ-uhnd)—a story handed down from earlier times

loch (LAHK)—the Scottish word for lake

ruins (ROO-ins)—the remains of something that has collapsed or been destroyed

witness (WIT-niss)—a person who has seen or heard something

Read More

Hamilton, Sue. *Air & Sea Mysteries.* Unsolved Mysteries. Edina, Minn.: ABDO Pub. Co., 2008.

Niz, Xavier. *The Mystery of the Roanoke Colony.* Graphic History. Mankato, Minn.: Capstone Press, 2007.

Walker, Kathryn. *Mysteries of Giant Humanlike Creatures.* Unsolved! New York: Crabtree Pub. Co., 2009.

Internet Sites

FactHound offers a safe, fun way to find Internet sites related to this book. All of the sites on FactHound have been researched by our staff.

Here's all you do:

Visit *www.facthound.com*

Type in this code: 9781429676373

Super-cool stuff!

Check out projects, games and lots more at
www.capstonekids.com

Index